Management Philosophy

Copyright © 2018 Wayne Franklin

All rights reserved.

Management Philosophy

Management Philosophy

Introduction	4
Aphorisms	6
Explorations	18
Confidential Data	18
Do the Due	19
Managing Remotely	20
Leading from Behind	22
Anecdotes	26
Overheating	26
Raises	27
Stepping Up	29
Conclusion	32
About the author	34
Why this book	35
Acknowledgements	38
Dedication	40

Management Philosophy

Management Philosophy

Introduction

This book has been kept very brief purposely. In fact, calling it a "book" is too generous. "Booklet" seems better fitting. The original intent was merely a few pages of aphorisms and to make these available to others seeking a better way to manage professionals. It was to be kept short and an easy read to encourage it to be read. When additional sections were added, this underlying principle was maintained to keep it imminently readable.

The booklet is divided into three sections: aphorisms, explorations, and anecdotes. It started as just a list of aphorisms which are little nuggets of wisdom, but a few points required more explanation so the explorations were added for these. As much as this author abhors anecdotes as too much filler, he understood he was very much in the minority. Therefore a few anecdotes were added to show some of these principles at work. Following the body of this work, a small section of self-aggrandizement is included, largely to satisfy employers of the genetic fallacy, answering "Who is this guy?" to some very small degree. (One likes to think he is more than a blurb.) On the other hand, perhaps others have had similar career paths and can identify with the desire to improve upon corporate management's all-too-typically self-serving philosophy.

Lastly—this caveat is offered with significant disgust that it's at all necessary—note the masculine gender has been used when referring to an unknown or hypothetical individual out of proper respect for the English language. Its longstanding rules exist to insure a common understanding so communication may take place effectively. If the reader instead sees bigotry herein or is otherwise offended, this author doesn't care even a little bit. The reader owns his own feelings and is free to choose offense or to receive the information as intended.

Management Philosophy

Management Philosophy

Aphorisms

What follows are aphorisms for managers, presented in no particular order. Contrary to the author's natural preference to present information in a top-down fashion, this shotgun approach is taken in hopes that it may paint a more complete picture and engage the reader's inferential reasoning to help it take root more effectively (if the reader will forgive the wildly mixed metaphors).

Trust but verify. (Ronald Reagan)

Do due diligence.

"I'm from Missouri" (the "show me" state) means empiricism always trumps theory.

Work as if everyone were watching. Decide as if The Judge were watching.

Strive with herculean effort to avoid becoming not the appearance of delay but the real cause of delay,

Authority without responsibility is tyranny. Responsibility without authority is slavery.

Multiply yourself by mentoring then delegating.

Always work yourself out of your job by raising leaders in your team toward doing your job, else you can't move on to bigger and better jobs yourself.

Let others speak until they prove they're going astray and then only minimally to guide.

Management Philosophy

It's not about you. It may be about the business, your team, the bottom line, the customer, or just what is right, but it's not about you.

As much as is ethical, be transparent and forthright.

Maintain confidences. Request permission to do otherwise.

A manager is a counselor, a teacher, an unreciprocated friend, and lastly a boss.

Follow up and follow through, or else follow down and follow out.

Do the one thing few others are willing to bear: decide. Then own it, success or fail.

Let others succeed or fail on their own, but empower them to succeed.

Expect from your team just a bit more than they can deliver, then encourage them relentlessly and celebrate their successes.

Never ask your team to do something you're not willing to do yourself.

You are never too good for any task.

It's called "work" for a reason. If you don't go home tired, you didn't work.

No excuses. Period.

Never give cause to be defensive.

Management Philosophy

Defend truth and righteousness, not yourself.

Be passionate. Be energetic. Celebrate victories. Mourn defeats. It's not just a job but a meaningful pursuit.

Work is a large portion of one's life, but it is not life. Stay balanced and insist upon the same in your team.

Don't speak like a manager, executive, or businessman, but like a real person. You may be in a position of authority over others, but you're not better than they. Setting yourself apart from them with a corporate facade tells them you no longer empathize with them. Be real. Be grounded. Be you, foibles and all.

Be straight with your team. If something sucks, say so. Don't sell them a bill of goods, as they won't buy it. Start from reality, however bad it may be, and build from there.

Tell your team what you are thinking but only after you are sure of your thoughts.

Share your concerns (about the organization, the future, whatever), but don't go so far as fear.

Your team's confidence comes at least partially from you, but yours must be genuine. If you lack confidence, go find it. If it's not to be found, be frank about that.

When asked, tell your team what you truly think. If you don't like the way things are going, say that. Then move quickly to doing something about it, making the situation better together.

If you never complain about a boss' plan that you dislike, your team will never believe you when you really do like one.

Management Philosophy

Don't ever lie. If you can't reveal something yet, just say that.

Your team's futures are in your hands. They must be able to trust you with them, and you must earn that trust by never betraying them. Once you've earned their trust, they will go to the ends of the earth for you.

When you make mistakes, admit them readily. When you're not mistaken, stand steadfast.

Stay grounded in reality, dispelling belief, desire, and bias, and you can't be wrong.

Everyone is a salesman. Every interpersonal interaction is a sale. Provide the facts. Show the need. Offer the solution. Make the case.

Multitasking can be done but at the expense of depth of concentration. Know when each is needed and don't be fooled into thinking the former suffices for the latter.

Challenge your team to grow, but remember to offer encouragement, too.

When rewarding achievements, make it a pleasant surprise, be it in timing or kind or magnitude.

Intermittent reinforcement is more effective at conditioning preferred behavior than consistent rewarding. Keep the rewards somewhat unexpected or even occasionally random, not predictable and therefore stale.

Be fun. It may be work but it can also be fun.

Management Philosophy

If you lose your sense of humor—whether dry, wry, sardonic, or silly—you lose your soul.

Team outings mustn't be part of the job but organic happenstance. Time at work, be it in the office or out, is still time away from competing priorities. The outing you intend as a reward may be seen by some as just more work. If the reward involves time, give it to them freely so they can spend it as they wish.

If the company won't offer any tangible rewards, fund them yourself as you're able. A good team makes your life and must not be taken for granted.

Never let the job come between an employee and his family, for he works only for them.

Be grateful. Your team does not need to work for you. They choose to. Thank them daily for all manner of contributions.

If you see an issue without an owner, get it one. If you can't find one, be one.

Embrace responsibility and accountability.

Business is business, not charity, inclusion, social justice, moral posturing, or bringing your dog to work. If business isn't tended first and foremost, eventually there will be nothing left for charity, inclusion, social justice, moral posturing, or bringing your dog to work. Let business tend to business, and all the many employees who also live outside of business hours may tend to charity, inclusion, social justice, moral posturing, and dogs.

Management Philosophy

Institute formal reward programs for non-managers based upon realized inspirations, those beyond job responsibilities, for earnings and savings. There's no cost to the company to share a percentage of the otherwise unrealized earnings and savings as a large, tangible reward for the inspired. For example, a software engineer comes up with a new market for an old product, or a janitor finds a unique way to prevent magnetic media from wearing out as fast. One recommendation is ten percent of first-year realized earnings/savings, no matter how large that bonus check becomes.

Remember your team, boss, coworkers and partners, and family are human beings, the supreme life forms and only moral agents on the planet. Treat them all with the respect they are due by virtue of their humanity.

The act of work is the process of choosing the logical over the emotional, but never forget people are emotional beings nevertheless.

There is a time to avoid conflict, when it will not accomplish anything positive, and there is a time to embrace conflict. Often the only way to resolve conflict is to push through it.

When dealing with interpersonal conflict, there can be no true and lasting objective resolution without first addressing the obscuring emotional pressures. Address the humanity of conflict first, then work on the factual problem beneath. Neither can be addressed successfully without addressing both and in their proper times.

Pursuing perfection will not result in achieving it but will result in continuous improvement.

Management Philosophy

First seek to perfect yourself, then offer the same to your team as they are able to receive it. Push but only gently and when welcome.

The top man sets the culture, tone, values, and ethics. For your team, as much as possible, be the top man.

Ignoring legal definitions to the contrary, the business is not a separate entity unto itself. Businesses are people. Customers are people. Vendors are people. Users are people. Every business is a people business. Business cannot be conducted except by, with, and for people.

Business is warfare, with managers as officers.

Pick your battles, ones that can be won, but do not shy from any battle that may be needed to achieve strategic goals.

Study Sun Tzu, for <u>The Art of War</u> applies to business as much, albeit metaphorically more often than not.

Better an abundance of information than a dearth. Learn and teach how to process copious information effectively and efficiently.

Learn to read fast to aid in processing information. Aim for 1000 or even 2000 words per minute with full comprehension.
1. *The first principle of speed-reading is to keep it visual only. Do not read "aloud" in your head but simply see the words and their meaning mentally.*
2. *The second principle of speed-reading is to widen your field of view to take in more words at any given moment, up to a full page at a time, letting your mind rearrange them properly and in real-time without having to take them in one at a time or even sequentially.*

Management Philosophy

> *(This mental ability is, for example, how you don't usually recognize the*
> *the same word repeated at the end of one line and the beginning of the next line.)*

Learn to type fast to aid in generating information. Aim for 100 words per minute or better with no mistakes.
  1. *The first principle of typing is to divorce eyes and hands. You may use a reference photo of the keyboard placed nearby while learning, but you mustn't ever look at your hands.*
  2. *The second principle of typing is to think/type in terms of real words and phrases, not letters. Do this by typing actual language, not those historically horrible typing class lessons ("asa asa asa sas sas sas"—argh!).*

When hiring, skill-matching is a distant second to aptitude. If the candidate can learn and adapt, skills can be developed easily. If the candidate can't adapt well, having matching skills at the outset will only be a short-term solution (arguably appropriate for contractors more than employees).

Co-location is a big deal. It's not that remote teams can't be made to work, but the benefits need to outweigh the costs.

In managing remote teams, start with a primary contact and team leader at the remote site to insure at least one person has the full picture. Expand communication paths organically from there, rather than limiting it to that one contact.

Manage employees where they are. Don't expect more than they can deliver. If they are professionally immature, manage them more closely. If they are more mature, encourage greater self-management. In all cases, teach them how to grow toward self-management and then leadership.

Management Philosophy

Firing is a last resort, an admission of failure in leadership, either in the employee's hiring or in his subsequent performance management or in his placement. If an employee must be dismissed in the end, do not hesitate to do so (with all due documentation etc.)... then fix whatever management process permitted such a failed employee.

Mistakes happen but they ought not happen more than once.

Lessons learned from mistakes should be visible as changes in process, tools, or people (e.g., growth and/or placement).

New team members should be culturally mentored, as it takes time to acclimate to a manager's established team culture.

The management chain of command should be respected.

Truly effective leadership is always "from behind", not dictatorial.

Leaders must not forget that following is a choice.

Leadership is not declared but earned, not taken but requested and permitted.

Intelligence is no substitute for knowledge, wisdom, and humility.

Meetings are for group communication and real-time collaboration, not filling timeslots. Minimize resource waste: fewer and quicker meetings, start and end on time, invite just those who need to be there. Maximizing communication and collaboration need not mean maximizing meetings.

Management Philosophy

Favor dynamic, real-time communication when collaborating. Drop by instead of phoning. Call instead of messaging. Message instead of email. Email instead of writing documents.

Favor documented, non-interruptive communication when archiving. Call instead of visiting. Message instead of calling. Email instead of messaging. Document instead of emailing.

Invest in relationships. Invest in people. Care about their lives. As a manager, insure your team knows they can count on you beyond just the job.

Do the cost-benefit analysis. Learn to do this quickly and intuitively when time is of the essence, but gather the data to back it nevertheless.

Welcome criticism when offered, as it's a sign someone else is investing in you for your betterment. Be open to criticism but don't request it out of insecurity.

Managing is like parenting, or at least it ought to be. Care about your team, invest in them, show them how to succeed, and you will share their glory when they do.

Remain faithful to truth.

Show integrity. Do what you say. Be on time. Don't lie. Deliver as promised. Consistently demonstrate your word is good.

Look for opportunities to do more. By delegating and empowering, then multiplying yourself, owning and improving becomes an ever growing habit.

A manager must not favor his own team so much that all others are prejudged as inferior.

Management Philosophy

It may be difficult to promote the best employees to leadership positions, for such employees are hard to find, but if they're also great leaders, their promotion will have a multiplicative effect.

There tends to be two kinds of employees, those who want to do a good job and those who want to do just the minimum. The former can enjoy freedoms like flexible hours, working from home when needed, running errands during the work day, and the like without much concern about abuse. The latter should be weeded out as early as possible, preferably before hiring. Don't let a few bad apples ruin it for the rest.

If any of these aphorisms borders on plagiarism by lacking proper attribution, note it was quite unintentional and should be taken as a compliment that inspiring authors of yore took root so effectively in this author's psyche that they can no longer be distinguished from his own thoughts. Send this author any such charges and future editions will see correct attributions.

Management Philosophy

Management Philosophy

Explorations

One-liners are helpful as tips and reminders, but some management philosophies call for deeper treatment.

Confidential Data

One of the most important functions a manager can provide both his team and his employer is shielding his team from his boss' failings. Everyone has failings, but a boss' failings inevitably affect the entire team adversely. When a boss does not have sufficient confidence in the leadership ability of a manager reporting to him, this boss may be inclined to meddle, even micromanage, the manager and his team. Since this boss is another layer removed from what the manager's team is doing, he is less likely to micromanage well (as if there were such a thing as micromanaging well). However, this is a natural reaction to a lack of confidence by the boss in the manager reporting to him.

The manager must garner his boss' confidence quickly to give him reason to back off. Knowing the project, the people, the processes, and the goals well certainly helps, but these are usually known by everyone on the team so they must not be enough. In any job, there is data. It could be the number of outstanding issues, categorization of features, timelines and schedules, costs and revenues, or any number of other sources of data. When there is qualitative uncertainty, quantitative certainty goes a long way to earning confidence. The manager must give his unsupportive boss data.

By presenting hard data gleaned from reality, there can be no argument against the manager's claims of having things under control. The data itself may not in fact prove the manager knows what to do, especially if there's not enough history to show his track record. However, even data that shows a problem is helpful as it demonstrates to the boss that the manager at least

Management Philosophy

understands the problem and its magnitude. This is a crucial first step, if nothing else. The next would be presenting a quantifiable plan to address the data, with milestones, where more collected data will show his progress.

When there is sufficient data collected for the manager to earn his boss' confidence, there will be little to no reason for any further micromanaging. Some historical patterns of this should cement the boss' confidence and free the manager to lead his team as he sees fit. After all, the data shows he knows what he's doing and that it's working for the company.

Do the Due

Due diligence is sometimes difficult to coax out of creative types, but it is a crucial philosophy to both success and proper recognition of the same. The digital age was to usher in the paperless era, but it just moved the paperwork online. For any task, issue, or procedure, there is surely paperwork to be done to define it, track it, and resolve it. A successful manager will do this due diligence and see that all the i's are dotted and t's crossed. There can be no argument of status when paperwork reflects reality correctly, and the paper trail insures the right team gets the credit.

Another benefit to completing the paperwork is insisting others do the same. If there's a formal process, this holds others' feet to the fire to make sure they do their jobs properly, too. In the spirit of leading from behind, insisting upon the process and its paperwork is sometimes the only leverage a manager of one team may have over other teams not in his reporting structure. A smart manager will use this to his team's advantage. Again, pertinent to the credit, this also insures blame is not wrongly assigned to the manager's team but to the team failing to do their due diligence.

Due diligence is also seen in following through in ways not related to paperwork. If an employee has a theory about a

Management Philosophy

problem's root cause, for example, the manager should insure he proves it. This is not a statement on the manager's mistrust in his employee's expertise but a matter of gathering irrefutable evidence for doubters outside the group to be silenced. Make this kind of due diligence a habit, and it will just become part of the usual process, a good and well practiced discipline.

Managing Remotely

One of the greatest challenges for a manager is managing remote resources. They may be in another location but close to the same time zone, or they may be so far away that there is no overlap in working hours (as is common with offshore teams). The value of collocation cannot be overstated, and there can be very large, hard to quantify costs associated with losing this important team trait. Nevertheless, there are ways to mitigate the costs of managing remote teams.

One of the most critical keys to managing offshore teams successfully is to have a primary contact at the remote site who has earned the manager's trust and confidence. The best way to achieve this is to bring the resource to the manager's site for in-person training and acclimation to the management culture. He needs to see the manager's work style and management style to fully understand what will be expected of him and his remote team.

The remote team then works for that key offshore leader so the manager's expectations can be transmitted transitively. To help insure this is happening, regular status reports should be expected of the remote team leader to the manager, including reports from each of the remote team members. The manager needs to get a feel for how the remote team is performing so corrections can be made.

Any corrections the manager needs to make to the offshore team should be done through that trusted offshore leader. Allow that leader to interact on a daily basis with the remote team in

Management Philosophy

ways familiar to the local culture, provided the management culture is respected. The remote leader should be treated as an integral part of the manager's team every bit as much as any of the manager's local employees. By extension, the remote team must be treated as part of the manager's larger team as many as any who are local. Periodic meetings with the remote team should be done, preferably with video conferencing or telepresence technology, to humanize not only the offshore team members but also the manager and his local team.

Maximize overlapping work hours whenever feasible. Oftentimes remote teams may have their work day skewed by only a few or several hours relative to the local manager's time zone. If working a bit earlier or later can help improve real-time interaction, encourage it. The worst case scenario is a 12 hour difference between teams. In such cases, there will need to be evening meetings, perhaps alternating which site takes evenings and which takes mornings, to keep the teams tightly integrated (e.g., 9pm/9am). Make sure it's well known that this "after hours" time is considered part of the normal hours for the week, not expected overtime. If the manager can make this sacrifice alone without involving his local team, he should do so. If the greater local team must attend for the sake of integration, then use whatever incentive or reward can be offered to make this more palatable.

The hardest situation is non-overlapping work days and a remote team made of inexperienced employees. More oversight is required with the professionally immature to help them learn what it means to be professionally mature and conform to management's culture. Stay close to the remote team to guide them. Stay connected more often. Insure greater awareness of expectations and feedback. When growing remote teams, grow them only as fast as employees can be integrated into the management culture successfully, relying on the veterans to train up the newer ones.

Management Philosophy

Encouraging a culture of energized excitement, fast action, and recognition and reward can go a long way to keeping a remote team well engaged. Keeping them tightly integrated with the local team helps them feel a part of the larger organization and not orphaned or, worse, forgotten. Offshoring, or any kind of non-collocated structure, has many challenges. The benefits may be largely in reducing labor costs or in working with remotely located partner businesses, but these may be enough to warrant the management costs. Despite being suboptimal, these above tips help make these conditions successful.

Leading from Behind

"Leading from behind" is a phrase popularized several years ago in the business community. The one preferred by this author is "the tail wagging the dog," but the sentiment is the same in this context. A related popular term is "change agent," as in "we should all become change agents." Traditional management philosophy, as practiced if not preached, taught that a manager's sphere of influence was largely limited to his own team, his subordinate organization. Leading from behind, or being a change agent, is a recognition that individuals can influence far beyond their station or authority.

A software manager does not manage the project management team or the hardware engineering team or the test team or the customer support team or the executive team. Even so, a software manager can influence the behavior and practices of all these other teams, up to and including pushing continuous improvement initiatives.

For starters, business is people and business is relationships. The organizational chart may not have all these disparate groups reporting to a software manager, but they all must work together toward common goals. As such, there are interactions, dependencies, status reporting, and more. Investing in the people in these other teams, getting to know them, helping them

Management Philosophy

whenever feasible, even casual watercooler chats can have a payoff more tangible and substantive than these investments.

If a manager is known to exhibit integrity, his character will be known by those outside his own team. When he comes knocking with a request, others will know he's not trying to get them to do his job but that his need is genuine and reasonable. When he is known to be grounded in reality, even his most fantastic plans are accepted as achievable. When he gladly embraces responsibility and ownership and is known to do so, his attention to a problem in another's group is not perceived as blaming or deflection but an earnest attempt to help the company do better. Character is everything. A manager with character above reproach can accomplish so much more than one known to serve himself first and foremost.

A conscientious manager first must get his own house in order. If he and his team aren't running on all cylinders yet—this metaphor starts to lose significance in an EV world—nobody on other teams is going to listen to criticism. If he fixes his own team's work, though, he not only has standing but proof it can be done. Showing how continuous improvement was implemented successfully in his own group can be a powerful motivator to others. It shows it can be done. It offers a competitive opportunity. It raises the bar for the manager's role. It restores some excitement to a job that may have otherwise become mundane and repetitive.

Passion for one's job is catching. We all have to work to put food on the table, but we'd all prefer to work at something that is fulfilling, meaningful, and fun. A manager who has mastered these traits on his own team can "infect" his peers similarly, thereby providing impetus for other teams to become more fulfilling, meaning, and fun, too. Doing the right thing can also be a passion, and most people prefer the opportunity to do the right thing if their cynicism can be overcome. Passion for doing what's right, and showing how it's best for the employees,

Management Philosophy

employer, and customers, can raise the performance of all who observe and are inspired.

Once several teams and their managers are striving for improvement, offering tips and even criticisms becomes a welcome activity. Output increased another five percent when it was previously thought impossible becomes an opportunity for glory and celebration. Rooting out inefficiencies and waste becomes a game of one-upmanship. A feedback loop of excellence is created.

Challenging the status quo (for it can always be better) can be done by anyone in any domain. A manager inspiring such a growth culture is respected enough that his suggestions can influence even presidents and boards of directors. It takes time and investment of heart, but one's designated role has little to do with how much he can contribute to a business. He becomes a change agent, the tail that wags the dog, a leader from behind, all without position-based limitation.

Management Philosophy

Management Philosophy

Anecdotes

Although this author prefers to avoid anecdotes of applications of a principle, most readers prefer these tangible examples of philosophy at work.

Overheating

A manager of a software team on a critical product development project, one to make or break the company, starting getting word from the customer about overheating devices. With hundreds of thousands of units deployed already and millions to come, an overheating problem stood the chance of killing the product's sales and ending the company within months. It needed to be managed carefully yet transparently.

This war had battles on several fronts. Internal pressures forbade the manager even to mention the word "hardware" when talking of this overheating problem, lest the device be blamed for a design flaw. Secondhand reports from the field suggested an overheating problem at a failure rate large enough to undermine customer confidence. Conversations were being held between executives of the customer's company and the product developer's company, conversations focused on this potentially critical problem. Naturally yet not helpfully, the status meetings and reports were requested so frequently as to prevent any actual work on the issue itself.

The manager needed to get the executives off his team so they could investigate the veracity of the customer's claims and the root cause of the overheating problem. He put together a synopsis of all the claims, who made them, what the numbers were, how the symptoms were described. It was a useless summary in itself, but it put all the known data in one place. This got the manager's bosses off his back just enough for him to deal with the issue. He also made it clear his team was his team, that his bosses were to work through him and not try to

Management Philosophy

manage his team or go around him. By demonstrating he had the problem well and correctly identified, confidence was earned and they backed off. The executives enjoyed discussing the synopsis itself, thinking they now knew what was going on, and kept themselves entertained for a while.

Meanwhile, back channels of communication were developed between the manager and the customer's low-level but key project players. This enabled him to ignore the executives' mischaracterization of the problem and the associated hysteria and get to the truth of the matter. It turned out, the root of the problem was that nobody knew what typical temperatures were supposed to be, so they didn't really know if anything was overheating.

By doing several targeted what-if tests and providing pretty charts of temperature changes under various conditions (data!, due diligence!), the manager and his team were able to placate the customer and his own executives. There was no crisis after all. All talk about the "overheating problem" cooled down.

Raises

The manager's favorite time of year was coming, raises. He had a great team and enjoyed the opportunity to reward their superior performance with increases in their base salaries. The overall economy was on the rise, and pay had been raised in numerous sectors and businesses. The division in which the manager worked overcame seemingly impossible hurdles and outperformed all peers. All expectations were that raises would be returning to the glories of yesteryear.

Word came down from on high that the budget for raises was a mere two percent. It was pathetic, given the team's performance, to say nothing of the overall economy. It turned out the superior performance of his division was being used to prop up the rest of the business, so his team was essentially punished for poorer performance elsewhere. Still, the manager

Management Philosophy

laid out his plans for raises for his team, proudly correcting some underpaid employees to more market competitive levels and rewarding them as much as possible.

His pay increase plan for his team was approved by his boss, his boss' boss, and so on, until it made it to the president. What should have been a rubber stamp then became a nightmare. The president send word to all of management that there would be no raises at all, citing "cash flow" as the reason. There was no explanation for how the pay-raise process had proceeded so far without cash flow being a problem or how how it had suddenly become a problem at the eleventh hour. No offers were made to aid in reward or retention, meaning critical talent was at risk of leaving the company for myriad reasons (low pay, no raise, no reward for a year of busting butt, etc.).

The manager was put into a bad position. Did he reveal to his team what had happened, or stay silent and offer no explanation or even announcement for the lack of raises this year? He decided to be transparent and forthright, sitting his team down and explaining everything that happened. Despite multiple flight risks, nobody quit. They were disappointed, of course, but they appreciated their manager's honesty and attempts to fight this unjust decision.

The team was not surprised by the lack of raises and did not hold the manager responsible. Had he remained silent, though, he could have been held personally responsible. Instead, he earned their loyalty even in spite of the economic disappointment. Under prevailing management philosophies, this outcome would not have been predicted, and the manager's transparency would have been condemned.

Even in the face of executive decree, the manager went to battle for the team. If he couldn't get all the raises he wanted for this team, maybe he could get a subset approved. Maybe the most grossly underpaid employees could at least get the reward and market correction they so sorely needed. It took another two

Management Philosophy

or three months of fighting executives with data, but one critical raise was indeed finally approved.

Stepping Up

A team leader, not yet promoted to manager, saw a long-term opportunity to promote project cross-training, expand awareness of employees, and improve resource mobility. These goals provided the team leader's boss' team with the ability to react more quickly and effectively to bursts of demand, crises, and changing market requirements. To start, only a single simple action was needed to get this ball rolling.

The team leader called a regular meeting with the boss' other team leaders and managers to discuss hot issues, resource needs, and business concerns. The boss was invited as an optional attendee just to keep him in the loop, but his presence was not needed for these purposes. The managers and team leaders were self-empowered to move people around the projects as needs required, and the boss was then updated with the plan and given the opportunity to veto it if he had other ideas coming from his larger business perspective.

The managers and team leaders also discussed any project risks, business problems (bill of material costs, deployment rates, purchase order declines, etc.), and even personnel desires (in case someone was looking for a new challenge). As a management team, they worked to resolve their separate issues together with what they collectively had at their disposal. Their boss was kept informed of their concerns and actions to address those concerns. As they became collectively self-managed, the boss' confidence in their abilities grew and he was freed to concentrate on larger concerns (earning new business, long-term cost controls, and so forth).

The team leader who began this superteam self-management initiative had no official authority to do any of this. He had no official position as a manager. He didn't even ask permission

Management Philosophy

but simply saw a need and a way to fulfill it without usurping any undue authority or costing the company anything. He was soon promoted to management officially, of course, since he had already demonstrated his ability to do the job.

Meanwhile, this new manager was working to move his high performing team members into de facto leadership roles in their own right. He helped them to learn how to multiply themselves and delegate their formerly unique expertise to others on the team. In this way, authority and responsibility was gradually pushed "downward" (from manager to team leader to subject matter expert to junior contributor to contractor). By doing so, the manager was increasingly available to take on more responsibilities (and authorities) that were formerly maintained by his boss. By taking more of his boss' duties--starting with the more mundane and less critical work--the boss was made increasingly available to concern himself with larger matters of the business. Everyone in the organization moved "upward" in responsibility, and the overall productive output of the whole organization increased.

Management Philosophy

Management Philosophy

Conclusion

This author's research showed, above all else, there is a single root cause of almost all of the ills in today's management structures, solipsism. It may be seen as self-centeredness, self-interest, self-preservation, narcissism, and even sociopathy. As these evils pile up via bad management, the end results tend to be a disregard for other human beings, undermining corporate goals or purpose, unethical behavior, regulatory and legal infractions, or outright scandal and notoriety. In stark contrast, good management requires moral grounding, selflessness or even occasional self-sacrifice, empathy, righteousness, and a desire to serve.

It's no wonder management tends to be bad when it descends from man's nature. Good management, then, requires managers to overcome their nature and act from the very best they can muster. As stress tends to interfere with self-control, and management tends to bear greater stresses due to greater responsibilities and stakes, one can see how management would be pressured toward man's baser nature and therefore perform poorly. Avoiding this natural process requires individual managers to deal with stress well and be practiced at remaining righteous under stress.

Managing well is far from easy, since human nature is being partially denied in oneself yet accepted in others. When enough individual managers decide they're willing to make this effort, only then will corporate management stop being the butt of jokes and the source of so much grief for businesses and employees alike.

Management Philosophy

Management Philosophy

About the author

Wayne Franklin started his professional career in 1983 as a technician at a small technology start-up business, responsible for custom computer modifications, configuration, software installation, diagnostics, and his first professionally written program, an Intel 8088 assembly language utility to park the hard drive heads in preparation for shipping. Later, he became the first part-timer/co-op in IBM history to receive a cash award for outstanding performance. He served on a board of directors for a small technology business, directed its R&D department, and architected its next-generation product that lasted decades. He has enjoyed success in all his ventures, often in spite of his employers' management.

Having observed corporate management, including being subjected to it and even inflicting it upon others earlier in his career, Wayne has seen it all, with what-not-to-do being the most frequent and valuable lessons. After maturing beyond the idealistic, shocked, disgusted, cynical, and burned-out phases of professional development, he was finally ready to enter a management role once again, this time armed with 35 years of wisdom.

Determined to avoid the countless mistakes he'd come to expect from management and emulating the best traits of the very few good managers he had enjoyed over his career, Wayne put into action is his own unique style. It wasn't until he received numerous positive comments from subordinates, peers, and superiors alike about his unusual style that he fully understood how different it was from normal and how successful. There are no illusions that the management style or wisdom in this book are the end-all of leadership. In fact, he deems them just the start of a better way of leading and hopes others are inspired to break the mold of mediocrity and start new and better trends in corporate management.

Management Philosophy

Why this book

The author had multiple false starts into management over his career. Though arguably competent, the earlier forays were far from fulfilling or supremely successful but they served well as instruction. After years of stepping back and closely observing what did and did not work in others' management philosophies, as well as learning from own attempts and from countless books, one more brave attempt was made to transition into management. This time, he struck gold.

Taking over mid-project on multiple products under heavy, concurrent development for a world class customer was a trial by fire. His predecessor had resigned under the pressure. Engaging at breakneck speed, balancing more tasks than most CEOs, and in large part determining the success or failure of the billion dollar company with his projects, the author began to put into practice the many lessons learned over three and a half decades of professional experience.

In the end, the projects succeeded, and the company was saved for another several years (the life of those products). Better still, the author's teams, both direct and dotted-line, learned of another style of management they hadn't seen before, one they liked and saw as key to their collective and individual successes. It was with humble reluctance that the author began to process his team's feedback and accept he had done something few others had done. It wasn't the projects' success, for many projects succeed despite poor management, but success amidst hard times and, better still, enjoying the process along the way.

Occasionally long hours were required of his team but never demanded. Stresses were sometimes high but resignation was not considered by anyone on the team. Personal lives remained well cared for and balance maintained. With an executive team that did not offer support, even undermining the team at times, and customers notorious for unreasonable demands, the team

Management Philosophy

members still frequently expressed having fun at their jobs and looking forward to coming to the office each day.

Although still believing he has very far to grow as a leader, this author began to think it might be worthwhile to record his management style in hopes others may be inspired and the declining trend of management potentially, eventually reversed. Such high hopes could lead to undermining the source of Dilbert's humor, but it would be to the benefit of countless millions of employees and employers all struggling to find a better way.

Management Philosophy

Management Philosophy

Acknowledgements

Many thanks to my good friend, Gangatharan Ekambaram, who honored me as my protégé; to my great managers, Chuck Williamson and Tom Johnson; and to Richard Shirkness who was both my best manager and best friend. All four of these men challenged and inspired me as a manager and as a man.

A hearty thanks, too, to Juliana Franklin for helping me polish this booklet into something presentable.

Management Philosophy

Management Philosophy

Dedication

This work is dedicated to my patient and loving wife and daughter. They tolerated my long work hours and sometimes enormous stresses as I struggled with impossible conditions and learned to do what is right. I am eternally grateful for their support and pride in me.

www.ingramcontent.com/pod-product-compliance
Lightning Source LLC
Chambersburg PA
CBHW030519220526
45464CB00006B/2870